O of Ekklesia

A Christian Manifesto

Paul Bock

CONTENTS

Introduction

ACKNOWLEDGMENTS

Above all I thank my Savior and King. I look back on my life and am overwhelmed by how I do not deserve your love and mercy. Thank you for dying for me, and the gifts you have given. To my beautiful wife. Thank you for waiting for me, for all your support over the past years, and for your strength. You have been such a help in this little project. You truly are the essence of Proverbs 31, Forever and Always...To my dad for always being an example of what a man who continually seeks after the Lord looks like. My mom for your patience and prayers, even when I wore plaid pants. Thanks for all the late hours helping me with this. And my daughter, even now I see God working in you. I pray you grow to love him more each day, and are more of a light for Christ than I could ever hope to be.

INTRODUCTION

"I really long and look for an increase of the gifts and fruit of the spirit in the life of the Bride. There is no distinction between a Biblically well-educated person and a secularly well educated person except the content of their facts if the Holy Spirit is not at work. The Holy Spirit's gifts and fruit are what turned the world upside down. We need His work in the earth." Patricia Heart, Koinonia Institute.

I am not a writer nor do I pretend to be. I am a much better speaker. Because this is through text, you will not hear my intonation and this is probably going to be the shortest book you are going to read for awhile. However, my prayer is that you hear my heart. We are family in Christ; and even though I do not know you, you are precious to me. My desire is to see all believers fulfill the mission God has laid upon each of our lives.

I would encourage you to begin with Acts 17:11. Paul had gone from Thessalonica to Berea, and this is what he wrote of the Bereans, "Now these were more noble-minded than those in Thessalonica, for they received the word with great eagerness, examining the Scriptures daily to see whether these things were so." (NASB) My encouragement is to be a Berean, receive what is written with eagerness and an open mind, then take the time and pour over the scriptures for yourself. As I said this is going to be a fast read, but I hope you take the time to study everything and come to your own conclusions.

There is no other way to say it; too long we have stood by as this world turns to a wasteland. We scurry away from the battlefield in fear. Those of us with living water choose to hide in our caves and hoard the truth. The Messiah called us the light of the world. We are supposed to be a city on a hill that cannot be hidden. Instead, we maintain a flame the size of a candle hoping to God no one sees our light when we should be raging infernos illuminating every dark place we come into contact. How can we continue to ignore the carnage taking place right outside our doorstep? Our world is filling to the brim with the blood of children, widows, the thirsty, the hungry, the damaged, the lost, the sick, the abandoned, and the despairing.

What Micah Kinard of the band Oh Sleeper said, I ask of you now, "What keeps this family of fighters from facing the war that they were bred for?"(1)

Our time on this earth is short. This conflict is coming to a head. I pray this book sets fire to your hearts as believers with a renewed love for the King. I also pray this ignites a movement within the body of Christ to take the message, power, and gifts of Jesus to the world. At this point in history, we as the body of Christ can no longer afford to live in the shadows. We have been given the ministry of reconciliation, (2 Cor 5) are the light of the world, (Mat 5) and have been called to the Great Commission. (Mk 16)

1. Oh Sleeper (2007), *The Color Theft*, When I am God, Solid State Records

CHAPTER 1
Let's be Honest

This chapter may seem rough, possibly judgmental. Please know that is not my intent or my heart. My goal is to expose some things in love, set a base so all things may be built up from a foundation of truth, and launch us toward new levels in our walk with Christ. I love the saying, "If you throw a rock into a pack of dogs, the one that barks the loudest is the one that got hit." Maybe you feel this does not apply to you or your church. Great! What I pray is we all self-examine with the standard of God's word and be honest about where we are as the Ekklesia. Understand this also, I tie myself to all that I am writing and realize how much I have failed my King.

We look at the church within the pages of scripture. We see all they accomplish, all that is promised, all that we are called to in the service to our King, and where do we see this taking place today? Like me, you may feel in your Spirit that something is missing within the body of Christ. Yes, there are pockets of believers who are sold out for Jesus but they are few and far between. Right now stop reading, take five minutes and watch "Rare Footage of Chinese Christians | Secret Underground Church."(https://www.youtube.com/watch?v=z9dsb be4zXc) After watching these brothers and sisters we cannot help but ask the questions, "What have we missed? What is holding us back?" One word: Fear.

Let us be frank, we fear persecution. We fear for our jobs, our standing, and what people may think. Unfortunately, one who is walking out all that they are called to as a believer will experience some level of persecution. This is a promise, "All who want to live a godly life in union with the Messiah Jesus will be persecuted." (2 Tim 3:12)

The Gospel is an offense because in order to accept it we have to acknowledge our sin and fallen nature. Christ makes it clear, "Everyone who practices wickedness hates the light and does not come to the light, so that his actions may not be exposed." (Jn 3:20) We, as the light of the world bring exposure to the darkness and have the ability to show people true reflections of themselves. This is something the world does not want to see so persecution is to be expected.

In addition to the fear of persecution, God takes a back seat to our pursuits. One example is the contrast between the fervor with which we worship the Messiah and sports.

We go to church and usually begin with 15-30 minutes of praise. I do not say worship because there exists a stark contrast between praise and worship. We sit in the pews, sing the songs, and muddle through with no real emotion or passion. At times those who display their passion and fervor are looked at with an eye of judgment or annoyance. As we praise, few hands are raised to the God of Heaven who purchased us with His own death, and there is little to no pouring out of oneself into the glorification of the Risen King. Yet, when our favorite team is playing we will raise our hands in the air, yell, scream, and throw our hearts full force into the game for hours. This is not a slight imbalance; this is straight idolatry!

Finally, a message is given for about 15-30 minutes that stimulates the mind but will never be taken out to the world. The mind is tickled, but beyond that there is no real life application except for what is in it for us. We have completely diminished and debased scripture down to simple intellectual jargon that stimulates us so we feel good about who we are and our present situation. We have turned God into Santa Claus and scripture into a self-help book.

We have to remember this is a war. It is a spiritual battle and the costs are far beyond what we can comprehend. We must begin acknowledging this. How can we expect to bring the message of freedom to those around us when we are still bound by the very flesh to which we are supposed to die?

One of the biggest issues within the body is that we do not die to ourselves and are seldom taught to do so. The Apostle Paul wrote, "I have been crucified with Christ; and it is no longer I who live, but Christ lives in me." (Gal 2:20, NASB) We act as though we do not know we are new creatures, "Therefore, if anyone is in the Messiah, he is a new creation. Old things have disappeared, and look! All things have become new." (2 Cor 5:20) Where is the change? Where is the transformation? Where is the understanding that we are nothing, and Jesus through the Holy Spirit is working in and through us?

I read an astounding statement that I completely agree with after being in the church for 33 years. "In the early church if the Holy Spirit had been removed, 95% of its activities would have ceased. In today's church if the Holy Spirit were removed 95% of the activities would continue." (1) This should scare us!

We have become like the Pharisees of Jesus' day to whom He accused, "You examine the Scriptures carefully because you suppose that in them you have eternal life. Yet they testify about me. But you are not willing to come to me to have life" (Jn 5:39-40). We can learn and quote scripture, have grand understanding of all the "ologies," yet never have our lives changed. We have become carnally minded and hold Scripture low, not intellectually, but in application and pursuit of our relationship with our King. We pick and choose what we want to accept from the Scripture and shrug off what makes us uncomfortable or ignore the passages which disagree with our preconceived ideas.

It would seem God is held more as an acquaintance we met once and every now and then we hit the like button or post a comment to Him. He has become an afterthought rather than our essence. In Acts 17:6, believers held the reputation of "turning the world upside down" where they lived. Why? Because their whole lives were a reflection of what they declared and the relationship they had with the Lord. The unsettling part of this problem is that while most Christians believe we should evangelize and speak knowledgeably with non-believers, the vast majority of the body does not, and in many cases cannot carry out this task.

It is time for us to take Scripture for what it is, believe what it says, die to ourselves and carry out the Great Commission. Again family, this is not to beat up on us but to state where we are. The beauty of this is that once we realize where we are, we can see where we need to go.

1. Johnson, Bill. (2016). *Hosting the Presence*. Destiny Image Inc, Shippensburg, PA. Pg. 21

CHAPTER 2
Is God serious about what He has spoken through His Word?

Does it matter how we interpret scripture? Everything we believe must be rooted and grounded in the word of God. We cannot pick and choose what to believe, but must believe what the scripture actually says! Obviously there are idioms and metaphors so I am not saying God has feathers as in Psalm 91:4. But in order to establish how important it is to take the Word for what is written, let us examine some prophecies of the Messiah and their fulfillment.

The Gospel is defined by Paul in 1 Corinthians 15:1-4, "That Messiah died for our sins according to the Scriptures, He was buried, He was raised on the third day according to the Scriptures." The Scriptures in Paul's day were the Old Testament. We see the death of the Messiah by crucifixion in Psalm 22 and Isaiah 53. The type and foreshadowing of the Jewish Messiah in Genesis 22 with Abraham and Isaac are beautiful. In Genesis 22 we have a father offering his son as a sacrifice, and it is the first time the word love appears in scripture. In Numbers 21, the brass serpent is a foreshadowing of the crucifixion and its purpose. The serpent represents sin and brass represents judgment due to its ability to sustain fire. So when Israel looked at the figure they saw sin judged. Jesus uses this model during His discussion with Nicodemus to prophecy His own death in John 3:14.

The prophecies in the Old Testament relating to the three days from Christ's death to resurrection are not as clearly defined. Jesus himself points to Jonah as a foreshadowing of the three days, "For just as Jonah was three days and three nights in the belly of the great fish, so will the Son of Man be three days and three nights in the heart of the earth." (Mt 12:40) There are many three day periods in the Old Testament like the example of Jonah, Abraham and Isaac, and the *tola* worm of Psalm 22.

The weight of all these passages is incredible. They reveal the depth, beauty, and design of scripture, but more importantly the fact that God says what He means. To drive this home let us examine Daniel 9. Our concern is not the entirety of the 70 weeks but the 69 mentioned in verse 25.

> Know therefore and understand, that from the going forth of the commandment to restore and to build Jerusalem unto the Messiah the Prince shall be 69 weeks: the street shall be built again, and the wall, even in troublous times."
> (Dn 9:25, KJV)

The prophecy states there would be 69 weeks from the command to rebuild Jerusalem until the Messiah presented Himself. The word for weeks is understood as a 7-year period, much like we understand a decade to be 10 years. We also need to understand that the old calendars consisted of 360 days per year. Sixty-nine seven-year periods, with 360 days constituting a year, gives us 173,880 days. The decree to rebuild the city is found in Nehemiah. Artixerxes Longimanus gave this decree on March 14, 445 B.C. The day Jesus Christ rode the donkey, fulfilling Zechariah 9:9, presenting Himself as the Messiah and King of Israel occurred on April 6, 32 A.D. March 14, 445 B.C. to April 6, 32 A.D is 173,764 days. Add 116 days for leap years and it equals 173,880 days exactly. (2)

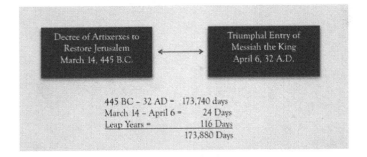

Decree of Artixerxes to Restore Jerusalem March 14, 445 B.C. ←→ Triumphal Entry of Messiah the King April 6, 32 A.D.

445 BC – 32 AD = 173,740 days
March 14 – April 6 =   24 Days
Leap Years =   116 Days
                      173,880 Days

Amazingly, after Gabriel prophesies the time when the Messiah will present himself, he states that the Messiah will be killed "but not for himself," (Dn 9:26) and after His death the city will be destroyed. Luke wrote that when Jesus came near the city He wept over it, saying,

> If you had known in this day, even you, the things which make for peace! But now they have been hidden from your eyes. For the days

will come upon you when your enemies will
throw up a barricade against you, and surround
you and hem you in on every side, and they will
level you to the ground and your children
within you, and they will not leave in you one
stone upon another, because you did not
recognize the time of your visitation.
(Lk 19:40-44, NASB)

Did this happen? Yes. The Romans in 70 A.D.
destroyed the city and the sanctuary. Why? Because
"you did not recognize the time of your visitation."
Jesus held Israel accountable to know Daniel 9 and
believe what was spoken. Are we honestly to think
we will be held any less accountable for what is
spoken in the scriptures since we have the Holy
Spirit to guide us into all truth? (Jn 16:13)

1. Missler, Chuck *Learn The Bible in 24 HRS notes*,
   Koinonia HouseInc, Coeur d'Alene, ID, pg.
   123

2. Sir Robert Anderson, The Coming Prince, pg. 96
   PDF.

CHAPTER 3
The Great Commission

God has implanted a deep compassion for the lost within the hearts of men throughout the ages. The ramification of an unsaved soul passing from this life to eternity is heartbreaking. The question is, why should you be concerned with evangelism? Should you be evangelizing? Are some called to be evangelists? Yes! Can you just live your life and let your actions speak instead of your words? No! Why? Because people are dying and going to Hell.

This fact is one we seem to ignore but it should absolutely break our hearts. Hell is a real place filled with real people. What I want is for you to imagine the person you love most in this life, the person who means more to you than anything, it could be a wife, child, parent, or friend. As you read the next two quotes I want you to stop reading and imagine them enduring this suffering with as much detail as you can create in your mind.

> Thus it is in Hell; they would die, but they cannot. The wicked shall be always dying but never dead; the smoke of the furnace ascends for ever and ever. Oh! Who can endure thus to be ever upon the rack? This word 'ever' breaks the heart. (1)

The torment of burning like a livid coal, not for an instant or for a day, but for millions and millions of ages, at the end of which souls will realize that they are no closer to the end than when they first begun, and they will never, ever be delivered from that place. (2)

The thought of that person who means more to you than anything enduring such horror should be almost unbearable. To what lengths would you go to save them? With what intensity and fervor would you work at keeping them from walking off that cliff into an eternity apart from God? We should be taking that passion and turning it towards all that are lost.

My fourth combat rotation was to Helmand Province, Afghanistan, in 2011-12. We were 27 days from coming home when my team was hit with a command detonated daisy chain IED that killed our EOD tech. For four months I had the opportunity to witness to him and I never said a word. I do not know if he would have accepted Christ, but the fact is, I never shared Jesus with him. I will never have another chance. No one is promised another day on this earth. So, while we are alive let us take every opportunity to share Christ because once this life is over everything is eternally set.

Ray Comfort is an evangelist who received the following letter from an Atheist and it is convicting to see the truth in the man's accusation.

You are really convinced that you've got all
the answers. You've really got
yourself tricked into believing that you're
100% right. Well, let me tell you just one
thing. Do you consider yourself to be
compassionate of other humans? If you're
right, as you say you are, and you believe
that, then how can you sleep at night? When
you speak with me, you are speaking with
someone who you believe is walking directly
into eternal damnation, into an endless
onslaught of horrendous pain which your
'loving' god created, yet you stand by and do
nothing.

If you believed one bit that thousands
every day were falling into an eternal and
unchangeable fate, you should be running the
streets mad with rage at their blindness.
That's equivalent to standing on a street
corner and watching every person that passes
you walk blindly directly into the path of a
bus and die, yet you stand idly by and do
nothing. You're just twiddling your thumbs,
happy in the knowledge that one day that
'walk' signal will shine your way across the
road.

Think about it. Imagine the horrors
Hell must have in store if the Bible is true.
You're just going to allow that to happen and

not care about saving anyone but yourself? If you're right then you're an uncaring, unemotional and purely selfish (expletive) that has no right to talk about subjects such as love and caring. (3)

The reality that people are going to Hell should put a fervency in us to share Christ however, what Jesus and the Father did for us should be an even greater driving force. We know what Jesus accomplished through His death and resurrection but I fear we do not fully comprehend the cost. First, Jesus became a man, not for His time on this earth, but for all eternity. He is still a man today. Three separate times after the resurrection Jesus appeared to His followers and they did not recognize Him: The Ameus Road (Lk 24), breakfast on the shore, (Jn 21) and Mary at the tomb (Jn 20). These were people who walked with the Messiah for years but they did not recognize Him. Why? Because He was unrecognizable.

In Isaiah 52 and 53 the prophet foretells the death of the Messiah, "Just as many were astonished at you, so was he marred in his appearance, more than any human, and his form beyond that of human semblance." (Is 52:14) What this means is that Jesus was so physically destroyed, He no longer appeared human. The prophet Isaiah also wrote, "I gave my back to those who beat me and my cheeks to those who pulled out my beard. I did not turn away my face from insults and spitting." (Is 50:6) This passage tells us Jesus' beard was ripped out as part of His torture. Where once these people saw a beard, they now saw scar tissue. That is the why his followers did not recognize Him, and it is the face we will look into when we are joined with Him.

In Revelation 5 a man is sought. John describes the man as a lamb that "looked like he had been slaughtered." (Rev 5:6, ISV) From Jesus' interaction with His followers and John's description in Revelation, we know He still bears the marks of His torture. As terrible as this is, the greatest torment our King endured on our behalf was the abandonment and wrath of the Father. That is what He endured for you, me, and everyone on this earth.

When we look at all Jesus bore on our behalf, the vastness of His love is easily seen. I do not want to take anything away from the Messiah. However, one thing we often miss when discussing the redemption is the love of the Father.

I remember when my wife was pregnant for the first time. The joy and the expectation were wonderful. I remember the first time I heard our child's heartbeat flood the room and saw the little body on the screen. In that instant I was overwhelmed with a love I had never experienced. I also remember a pain that is beyond description as we were told we were going to lose our baby. As they searched for a heartbeat and heard nothing come across the speaker, we were devastated. I would have gone to any length, up to giving my own life to be able to save our baby.

God in heaven watched as they tortured, mocked, spat on, destroyed, and crucified His son. Imagine the pain of the Father as He watched all this occur. The Father not only withheld intervention, but then poured His own wrath out on His Son. As a father I could not imagine pouring my wrath out on my daughter. It would crush me. Yet the Father did this in order to redeem us to Himself. I do not think we have the capacity to truly comprehend that depth of love.

After all this occurred, Christ gave us the Great Commission, "As you go into the entire world, proclaim the gospel to everyone." (Mk 16:15) This is not for the evangelist, but to the entire body. The word for proclaim or preach in the Greek means *after the manner of a herald.* If we remember from history a herald was one who would take a message from the kings or nobles and proclaim it to the masses. That is the intensity conveyed in the command. If you claim Christ, this is your calling as much as it is mine. As we walk through life we are to be continuously sharing the Gospel of Jesus Christ, and also what it is going to cost them if they reject Him. Think of all our King did for us through a love that withheld nothing. Why then do we hold anything back from Him and hold Him back from a dying world?

What is going to happen when we stand before our King to give an account for our lives? Will we look at Him and say, "God, I really tried to live the life you called me to by not sinning; I went to church, I tithed, and I treated people with kindness." I think He will look at us and ask, "That's great, how many people did you tell about me? Did you warn them about the path they are walking? What was the last command I gave you while I was on earth?"

Let me take some stress off. The best part about evangelism is the pressure is not on us to convert a person. We do not, nor should we try to force a conversion. Paul wrote, "I planted, Apollos watered, but God kept everything growing. So neither the one who plants nor the one who waters is significant, but God, who keeps everything growing, is the one who matters." (1 Cor 3:6-7) Our job is to sow seed and water. That is all!

1. Watson,Thomas cited by Pittenger, Norman. (1987) *Freed to Love: A Process Interpretation of Redemption,* Morehouse-Barlow, Wilton, Conn, Pg. 83

2. Whitefield, George cited by Hofstadter, Richard. (2004) *America at 1750: A Social Portrait,* New York: ACLS History E-Book Project p. 240

3. *Letter from an Atheist,* www.livingwaters.com

CHAPTER 4
How much should we pursue the Scriptures?

In any environment we need food for energy to carry out our tasks. In the military we have the meal ready to eat. The purpose of this meal is to pump calories into the soldier so he has the energy to fight. The consistency within the Bible is that the scriptures are spiritual food. Paul refers to the milk and the meat of the word in his letters. Jesus quotes Deuteronomy 8:3 when responding to the devil's temptations by stating that man lives not just by bread, "but by every word that proceeds out of the mouth of God." Do we go to get a handout from a person for our natural food once a week? Of course not! Then why do we seek our spiritual food once a week?

We should be studying, meditating, and memorizing scripture; not just giving God 5 minutes by doing a quick devotion and calling it good. We need to spend time learning what God has spoken to us. I love what my buddy Dave said, "Before, I just read the Bible because it is something you are supposed to do. But it finally made sense and I wanted to read when I realized it's God's half of a conversation."

The prophet Jeremiah wrote, "Your words were found and I ate them, and Your words became for me a joy and the delight of my heart; for I have been called by Your name, O Lord God of hosts." (Jer 15:16, NASB) The word for eat in the Hebrew means to eat or devour. As Jeremiah feasted on God's word it was a joy, a gladness, an exultation, and a rejoicing of the inner man or soul. It can be the same for us.

Being in God's word is vital to the believer in order to produce fruit. The Spirit through David wrote,

> Blessed is the man that walketh not in the counsel of the ungodly, nor standeth in the way of sinners, nor sitteth in the seat of the scornful. But his delight is in the law of the Lord; and in his law doth he meditate day and night. And he shall be like a tree planted by the rivers of water, that bringeth forth his fruit in his season; his leaf also shall not wither; and whatsoever he doeth shall prosper" (Ps 1-3, KJV).

This is an incredible promise, but a condition exists. The blessed man not only lives righteously but delights in and meditates on the scripture. Verse 3 gives us the ramifications of carrying out verse 2.

Just as is stated in Psalm 1, the Lord makes a similar promise to Joshua,

> This book of the law shall not depart from your mouth, but you shall meditate on it day and night, so that you may be careful to do according to all that is written in it; for then you will make your way prosperous, and then you will have success." (Josh 1:8, NASB)

Day and night they were to meditate on God's word in order to follow and carry out what was written. Then their way would be prosperous.

In ancient Israel, the king was required to write out his own copy of the Law. Moses wrote,

> Now it shall come about when he sits on the throne of his kingdom, he shall write for himself a copy of this law on a scroll in the presence of the Levitical priests. It shall be with him and he shall read it all the days of his life, that he may learn to fear the Lord his God, by carefully observing all the words of this law and these statutes, that his heart may not be lifted up above his countrymen and that he may not turn aside from the commandment, to the right or the left, so that he and his sons may continue long in his kingdom in the midst of Israel. (Deut 17:18-20)

Every day the king would read the Law to learn to fear the Lord. Reading it helped to keep the king from pride because God's law sheds light on our sin. (Rom 7) It is hard to become prideful when we realize how much we fail. Continually reading the Law also kept the king from turning away from God's commandments.

Just as this applied to the king of ancient Israel, it applies to us. If we are in the Messiah, we are Kings and Priests. (Rev 1:6, 5:10) We need to be in the scripture every day in order to not turn away due to how Jesus described the path we walk in this world. "For the gate is small and the way is narrow that leads to life, and there are few who find it." (Mat 7:14, NASB) Imagine walking through the woods on a dark night. The path is small and hard to see. We would use a light source to illuminate our way to ensure we stay on the path. The world we live in is dark and there are many opportunities to get off course. God gave us the light source to ensure we are able to stay on the path. The Psalmist wrote, "Your word is a lamp to my feet and a light to my path. (Ps 119:105, NASB) This is the reason it is crucial to keep the light before us.

Not only do we want to keep a light before us, we also want to maintain the light within us. Memorizing scripture aids in this process. David hid God's word in his heart in order to not sin against the Lord. (Ps 119:11) God promises that He will provide an escape when temptations arise.

No temptation has overtaken you but such as is common to man; and God is faithful, who will not allow you to be tempted beyond what you are able, but with the temptation will provide the way of escape also, so that you will be able to endure it." (1 Cor 10:13, NASB)

What is the way of escape? How do we resist the devil and cause him to flee? Psalm 119:11 is our guide. Jesus also gave us an example of this in action during His temptation by responding with scripture to everything Satan offered. (Mat 4:1-11)

An important point must be made here. Part of Satan's strategy when tempting Jesus was to use the scriptures. He had taken pieces of scripture and applied them on their own, apart from the rest of God's word. Although such application could sound logical, when compared to the whole counsel of God, such application is not only incorrect but sin. Satan's strategy is no different today; and our protection against such tactics is to remember two truths. First, "every fact is to be confirmed by the testimony of two or three witnesses," (2 Cor 13:1, NASB) which removes any justification for one verse theology. Second, Paul gave a prophetic warning,

For the time will come when they will not endure sound doctrine; but wanting to have their ears tickled, they will accumulate for themselves teachers in accordance to their own desires, and will turn away their ears from the truth and will turn aside to myths." (2 Tim 4:3-4, NASB)

Paul also encouraged Timothy to study and accurately handle the word of truth. (2 Tim 2:15) We must accurately handle God's word, steer clear of eisegesis, and be exegetical in our study. I would encourage you to read Gotquestions.org's short article about the difference between the two. Our guard against error and temptation is the entirety of God's word and for this reason we must be Bereans.

Paul wrote, "All Scripture is inspired by God and profitable for teaching, for reproof, for correction, for training in righteousness; so that the man of God may be adequate, equipped for every good work." (2 Tim 3:16-17, NASB) We are to use the scriptures to teach. Reproof means that by which a thing is proved or tested. Everything should be tested with the scriptures: Teachings, actions, attitudes, literally everything. Correction is to restore to an upright or right state. Training in righteousness means scripture is our guide on how we should live. The end state is for the believer to be mature and useful for the purposes of God. Walking all this out is Jesus' description of being a disciple.

Jesus said, "If you continue in my word, then you are truly disciples of Mine; and you will know the truth, and the truth will make you free." (John 8:31-32) It is not uncommon to hear someone say, "know the truth it will set you free." Unfortunately, the requirement in this passage to continue in His word in order to know the truth is often ignored. The Greek for continue means to remain or abide. We are to remain and abide in the word.

Many in the church seek to hear God speaking. Sometimes in seeking to hear God we do not pour over and search the scriptures because we have forgotten that God has already spoken to us through His word. Let this be a challenge, a call for us to devour the word of God.

CHAPTER 5
Worship

Let us not forget David whose heart of worship was so intense, he danced with all his might before the Lord, then basically told his wife, "you haven't seen anything yet." (2 Sam 6:16-23) David is called a man after God's own heart!

In the same manner that scriptures should be a daily part of our life, so too should worship. Worship is vital to the believer's relationship with the Lord. I can attest that it completely changed my prayer life and brought me to a deeper relationship with my King.

What is true worship? Is there a difference between praising the Lord and worshiping the Lord? Yes. We talk about worship, exhort others to worship and sing worship music, yet do not allow him to cleanse our hearts and change our lives.

Why did Christ come? Why was He conceived? Why was He born? Why was He crucified? Why did He rise again? Why is He now at the right hand of the Father? In order that He might make worshipers out of rebels; in order that He might restore us again to the place of worship we knew when we were first created." (1)

Worship is not praise but an act of total surrender to the Lord. The question must follow: how many of us know how to worship?

Each person of the Trinity is involved in the process of worship. To be spiritually cleansed requires reconciliation to God through Christ (Rom 5:9-11) and salvation. (Rom 10:9-10) If a believer has sinned purification comes by confessing sin to the Lord. (1 Jn 1:9) Only after the believer is fully purified can they enter a place of worship.

God can only be worshiped in spirit (Jn 4:23-24) and by the spirit the believer worships. (Phil 3:3) This requires the indwelling of the Holy Spirit who is sent from the Father. (Jn 14:16) Nancy Missler describes worship as "a uniting or a becoming one of two separate spirits. Worship means binding ourselves or joining ourselves to the object of our love. God is a Spirit and only that which is spirit can abide in His presence." (2) The Father is not only the supplier of the Spirit, but the object of worship.

Paul made the point that the believer is the same as Solomon's temple and houses God's presence. (1 Cor 3:16) The Psalmist stated it requires clean hands and heart in order to stand in the Holy Place. (Ps 24:2-4) God is the same today as He was during the days of Solomon (Heb 13:8) and is consistent.

(Js 1:17) Therefore, while the ceremony and ritual of the Law is now fulfilled in Christ, (Mat 5:17) the requirements of worship are still the same today.

Solomon's temple is unique in that it housed the presence of God. (2 Chron 5:13-14) It was also the only temple which held the Ark of the Covenant and the Mercy Seat. The Mercy Seat was a requirement for the presence of the Lord to manifest His presence. In heaven, God dwells between the Cherubim, (Is 37:16) and it was between the cherubim, over the ark of the covenant where God promised Moses He would meet them.

The people could praise the Lord at any point, however, a specific process took place for them to worship. The people would enter the outer court singing and praising the Lord. The priests then entered the inner court to wash their hands and feet. (Ex 30:18-19) Next, the priests sacrificed an animal on the brazen altar in order to remove the sin of the people. (3) After the sacrifice the priests immersed themselves in the Molten Sea, took coals from the Brazen Altar into the Holy place, changed clothes, took incense and dashed it over the golden incense altar. As they came near the altar, the priests removed their shoes, bowed down and worshiped the Lord.

What does this look like for us today? Just as in ancient Israel, there is a proper order we must follow for the believer to enter God's presence and worship.

Worship is "not an external ritual, but a bowing down and surrendering of ourselves internally." (4)

We are to enter His courts with praise and thanksgiving (Ps 100:4) like the priests in the outer court. Praise Him by reading the Psalms. Praise Him for who He is and what He has done. Thank Him for salvation, His love, His mercies, His continual grace and forgiveness.

After praise and worship, the priests entered the inner court and carried out the ritual cleansing. In like manner, before we can enter the holy place, we too must recognize and confess our sin. We cannot walk into His presence with unconfessed sin. Ask the Lord to reveal sin, confess and repent, forgive anyone who we have not forgiven and surrender the things the Lord has shown us. Once sin and self are put off we can then be received into God's presence.

> At this moment our spirits are united as we have put on His nature so we can now boldly go before the throne in the Holy Place. (Heb 10:19-22) Imagine carrying the coals of a surrendered life from the brazen altar into the Holy Place and incense altar where God has promised to meet with us. (Ex 25:22) Now we can truly worship him with clean hands and heart. This is when we bow down offering our love adoration and surrendered life. (5)

In this moment we must do as the Lord leads. We do not ask for anything, but simply adore and make Him the focus.

Imagine the change we would see in the body if we were to take hold of what true worship is and put it into practice collectively. What would church look like if an entire congregation came already prepared to worship? Even more importantly, what would your life and relationship with the Lord look like?

1. Tozer, A.W. (n.d.). The Very Best of Tozer. Retreived from ServantsoftheMessiah.org

2. Missler, Nancy. (2002) Private Worship: The Key to Joy, The KingsHighway Ministries, Coeur d'Alene, ID, Pg. 22

3. Orr, J. (n.d.). The Brazen Altar and Court of the Tabernacle. Retrieved from: http://biblehub

4. Missler, Nancy. (2002) Private Worship: The Key to Joy, The KingsHighway Ministries, Coeur d'Alene, ID, Pg. 37

5. Ibid, Pg. 110-111

CHAPTER 6
Kill the Man Inside

"It is no longer I who live but the Messiah in me." (Galatians 2:20) Everything in this book ultimately involves sanctification. Sanctification is the process of becoming holy and Christlike. It involves dying to self and allowing Christ to take over and live through us. This bleeds into every area of our life, from relationship with the Lord to relationships with others.

Paul called us to sanctification when he wrote,

> I therefore urge you, brothers, in view of God's mercies, to offer your bodies as living sacrifices that are holy and pleasing to God, for this is the reasonable way for you to worship. Do not be conformed to this world, but continuously be transformed by the renewing of your minds so that you may be able to determine what God's will is— what is proper, pleasing, and perfect. (Rom 12:1-2, ISV)

We have an active role in offering every part of our lives to the Lord for His use. We are commanded not be conformed to this world but transformed. (Rom 12:2) Dying to ourselves is a requirement.

Let me give you a warning: If you are going to pursue Jesus, work to die to self and be all that He desires, it will cost you. Jesus gave this warning when He stated the requirements of discipleship to His followers,

> If anyone comes to me and does not hate his father, mother, wife, children, brothers, and sisters, as well as his own life, he can't be my disciple. Whoever doesn't carry his cross and follow me can't be my disciple. Suppose one of you wants to build a tower. He will first sit down and estimate the cost to see whether he has enough money to finish it, won't he? Otherwise, if he lays a foundation and can't finish the building, everyone who watches will begin to ridicule him and say, 'This person started a building but couldn't finish it. Or suppose a king is going to war against another king. He will first sit down and consider whether with 10,000 men he can fight the one coming against him with 20,000 men, won't he? If he can't, he will send a delegation to ask for terms of peace while the other king is still far away. In the same way, none of you can be my disciple unless he gives up all his possessions. (Lk 14:26-33, NASB)

Jesus is not telling us to hate these people; that would be a contradiction. What He is saying is that our love for Him needs to be so great everything else in comparison looks like hate. He is also not calling us to give up everything we own. The Greek word for give up means to withdraw from, renounce, and forsake. Jesus is saying we must relinquish any hold that material possessions have over our lives. We need to count the cost because it will cost us; sometimes in ways we could never imagine.

In December 2013, I asked the Lord for an opportunity to minister to people with cancer and their families. What I did not know was at the same time my wife had been praying to be used by God and for new testimonies. At 4:30 in the morning, January 15, 2014, my wife, Kelsey, walked herself down to the emergency room after working all night. Four hours later she was diagnosed with acute myeloid leukemia. After a month of unsuccessful treatment at the University of North Carolina we were sent to M.D. Anderson in order for her to continue treatment, including a stem cell transplant. During that time we were able to minister, witness, and pray with others who were also fighting cancer. We saw miracles occur with Kelsey and other people. God answered our prayers to be used by Him, but not in the way we would have ever expected.

The whole process from diagnosis to coming home was about eight months. The next three years would be the most difficult time of our lives with Kelsey going through the recovery process, wondering if she was going to survive, and working through the emotional and spiritual consequences. We asked to be used by God and He honored that prayer, but it has cost us. We wanted a large family but we can no longer have kids naturally. For two years my wife was not allowed in the sun and even today must be careful. But what an honor to be used by God, to be counted worthy enough to endure something like this so that we could be a light to those going through the battle with cancer.

When we ask God to use us or tell Him we want to draw closer, He will begin to remove things from our lives. Many times the things removed are those with which we are most comfortable, but God removes them due to the fact that being comfortable can breed stagnation and apathy. In combat the fastest way to get someone hurt or killed is complacency. It is often painful as the Lord prunes and cuts away in order for us to grow in Him. Looking back, my wife and I now recognize God was pruning us for His purposes.

If you eagerly seek the Lord He will begin to work in you. When the process becomes painful I would not only encourage, but plead with you not to stop and back away. Dive headlong towards the Lord even if you are to the point where you feel God has abandoned you. It is at this point when faith matters most. It is easy to say we have faith during the peaks; but the valleys are where we are tested. A friend once said, "the mountain tops are great for views and recovery, but the valleys are where the fruit is grown." You have to believe that God is a good Father who only wants the best for you and desires to see you fully walk out His calling.

One of the best practices we can undertake in order to die to ourselves is fasting and prayer. This is a vital subject which significantly aids the believer in his walk with the Lord but is sorely neglected within the church. A true fast is not giving up television or chocolate, but depriving the body of food. I know many believers who struggle for years with breaking addictions in pornography, have temper issues, or whatever. If they were to fast and pray it would be amazing how quickly such issues could be overcome. Why? Because when we deprive the body of food, our body turns its attention to the fact that it needs sustenance. Everything takes a backseat because the body is trying to survive.

Fasting was not only for the early church, but also for the church today. Jesus was clear that He expects the believer to fast when He stated, "The time will come when the groom will be taken away from them, and then they will fast." (Mat 9:15, Lk 5:34, Mk 2:19-20) We fast to die to self. Fasting strengthens the spiritual man by weakening the physical. Prolonged fasts are incredible and I would challenge all believers to fast and pray for at least a week at some point. It is amazing what it can do for our relationship with the Lord. There are many faith based resources available regarding how to fast.

A word of caution about the end of a fast. Satan did not tempt Jesus at the beginning or during His fast, but at the end when He was most vulnerable. Satan will want to nullify everything accomplished during a time of fasting and prayer so we have to be prepared for the attack that may come.

CHAPTER 7
Our Rewards

We have covered very heavy topics, but what is there to gain or lose? What lies ahead for us as believers? How many Christians know we will be judged? These are serious questions because the ramifications of our judgment will be eternal and affected by all we have discussed.

Paul, in multiple letters, wrote about the judgment that believers will endure: "For we will all stand before the judgment seat of God...So then each one of us will give an account of himself to God. (Rom 14:10; 12, NASB) For we must all appear before the judgment seat of Christ, so that each one may be recompensed for his deeds in the body, according to what he has done, whether good or bad," (2 Cor 5:10, NASB) What we notice in these passages and others is that our actions and fruit are being judged, not our salvation. Paul described the judgment we as believers will undergo in detail,

> For no man can lay a foundation other than the one which is laid, which is Jesus Christ. Now if any man builds on the foundation with gold, silver, precious stones, wood, hay, straw, each man's work will become evident; for the day will

show it because it is to be revealed with fire,
and the fire itself will test the quality of each
man's work. If any man's work which he
has built on it remains, he will receive a
reward. If any man's work is burned up, he
will suffer loss; but he himself will be saved,
yet so as through fire. (1 Cor 3:10-15,
NASB)

Earlier in this chapter, Paul described those that
sow and water as nothing, however, each receives a
reward based on what they allowed the Holy Spirit to
do through them. Imagine a pile before every
believer. It will be built of elements representing
what we have done for the King and what we have
done for ourselves. Fire is going to be put to all we
have stored up and whatever remains is our
inheritance. Some are going to have an amazing
inheritance, while others will lose everything. As my
mom would sometimes say, "You made it through
the fire, but you've got smoke on your clothes."

I fear that many Christians will be disappointed
because we have been taught that all are equal and
that all will reign as heirs with Christ. But that is not
what the text says. Paul is clear,

The Spirit himself testifies with our   spirit
that we are God's children. Now if we
are children, we are heirs—heirs of God and
co-heirs with the Messiah if, in fact, we share

in his sufferings in order that we may also share in his glory." (Rom 8:16-17)

The word if, makes it clear that there is a condition in this passage. Sharing in Christ's sufferings can take many forms such as persecution, trials, and other endless possibilities.

A Christian brother in Africa comes to mind when I think about the judgment we as believers will endure. I heard him speak about His father's Christian orphanage in Africa. Once the children are of age, they have to leave the orphanage. Many go to the nearby city and are incredibly poor. This brother has moved from his father's orphanage to a one bedroom apartment in the city in order to help take care of these kids who have outgrown the orphanage. He lives there with his wife, children, and eight previous orphans who have since married and have children of their own.

How are we going to stand before our King and answer for the fact that we have spent hundreds of thousands, in some cases millions of dollars on buildings to meet for church, yet we did not help our brothers or sisters in these situations? Have we forgotten Matthew 25:40? "To the extent that you did it to one of these brothers of Mine, even the least of them, you did it to Me." (NASB) Jesus said, "Where two or three have come together in my name, I am there among them." (Mt 18:20) Francis Chan made a powerful point when he said,

We had this huge building project, you
know, some multi-multi-multi-million
dollar building project. This little village we
were going to build. I just looked and I
went, I can't do that. I don't think that's
how Jesus would have done it. I think
He would have said, "Just meet me at the
park." You know, and I said why don't
we just plant a bunch of grass and we'll meet
outside. And people were like, 'Well what if
it rains?" I'm like, "We'll probably get
wet." But we're in southern California
come on! And I go man haven't you ever
heard of the Green Bay Packers? People will
sit in a storm for four hours and pay money
to do it...But they'll do that, and we won't
sit in southern California weather? For an
hour and a half? To worship God? (1)

The location we meet does not matter, only that we
come together in the name of our King.

1. Chan, Francis (n.d.), If Jesus was your pastor you
probably wouldn't go to his church.
Retrieved from youtube.com.

CHAPTER 8
Brothers and Sisters

The fact of the matter is we are all part of the ultimate statistic: 10 out of 10 die. Are you saved by confessing with your mouth Jesus is Lord and believe in your heart God raised Him from the dead? (Rom 10:9-10) Have you turned from your sins and given your life fully to Christ? GREAT! What have you done with it? Once the day arrives when the Lord comes or calls us home, there are no more chances. Everything is eternally set.

I now ask the questions: Is Jesus what you really want? Have you counted the cost? If you have not, why? If not now, when?

I want to close with one of the most powerful professions of faith I have ever read. It has been attributed to a martyred African pastor after his death.

> I am part of the fellowship of the unashamed.
> I have Holy Spirit power, my die has
> been cast. I have stepped over the line.
> The decision has been made. I'm a disciple of
> Jesus. I won't look back, let up, slow down,
> back away, or be still.

My past is redeemed, my present makes
sense, my future is secure. I'm finished and
done with low living, sight walking, small
planning, smooth knees, colorless dreams,
tamed visions, worldly talking, cheap giving,
and dwarfed goals.

I no longer need pre-eminence,
prosperity, position, promotions, plaudits,
or popularity. I don't have to be right, first,
tops, recognized, or rewarded. I now live by
faith, lean on His presence, walk by patience,
am uplifted by prayer, and labor by power.
My face is set, my gait is fast, my goal is
heaven, my road is narrow, my way is rough,
my companions are few, my Guide is
reliable, and my mission is clear. I cannot be
bought, compromised, detoured, lured away,
turned back, deluded, or delayed.

I will not flinch in the face of sacrifice,
hesitate in the presence of the adversary,
negotiate at the table of the enemy, ponder
at the pool of popularity, or meander in the
maze of mediocrity. I won't give up, shut
up, let up, until I have stayed up, stored up,
prayed up, preached up for the cause of
Christ.

I am a disciple of Jesus. I must go till
He comes, give till I drop, preach till all
know, and work till He stops me. And when

He comes for His own, He will have no problem recognizing me.

My banner will be clear.

www.onslaughtofekklesia.com

49211408R00031

Made in the USA
Columbia, SC
19 January 2019